Daring Deeds

Stan Cullimore

Illustrated by
Paul Cemmick

OXFORD
UNIVERSITY PRESS

Contents

1 Dragon trouble

King Max and his son, Prince Oliver, were
playing on the computer. The prince had
just brought it back from his travels.

There was a knock on the door.

Two men came in, carrying the body of
a knight.

"Not another one," groaned the king.

"The dragon bit his head off," said one
of the men. The king sighed.

"Take him away. He's bleeding all over
the floor."

Prince Oliver looked worried.

"This is bad," he said and pressed "quit".

"But I think it's a great game . . ."
said the king.

"Dad!" said Oliver. "I mean that headless knight! What's been going on here?"

The king looked sheepish.

"We've had a spot of bother with a dragon," he said.

Oliver looked at the pools of blood and then at his father.

"Well, quite a lot of bother, actually," said the king.

The king explained how the dragon had woken up and flown down from the mountains. It was causing chaos. Oliver paced round the room. He could hardly believe his ears.

"I've only been away a month," he said. "But in that time the dragon has eaten our crops, drunk the rivers dry, burnt our villages, and snacked on the heads of our bravest knights!"

The king nodded.

"Why didn't you tell me what was going on?" asked Oliver.

"I lost your mobile number," said the king.

There was another knock at the door.
A boy stumbled into the room. His
clothes were black and burnt.
"The dragon . . ." gasped the boy.
". . . another village . . ."
Then he fell to the floor
in a smoky heap.

"Call for another knight," said the king.
"And then what?" asked Oliver crossly.
"Are you just going to keep sending our best
knights to their death?"

There was an awful silence. The king stood up. He went to his throne. He put his crown straight.

"I am the king," he shouted. "Everyone does what I say."

Oliver was not afraid.

"You may be king, but you still need help," he said.

"No!" shouted the king. "This is my kingdom and I am going to do what I want!"

"Here we go again . . ." said the prince.

Then a cunning look crossed the king's face.

"I've got an idea," he said. Oliver didn't feel too hopeful.

"In my book of *Daring Deeds*," said the king, "there's a very brave, bold knight. He's clever too. He can kill the dragon."

The king was smiling, but Oliver saw a snag.

"But that book is old," he said. "That knight will be old too!"

The king frowned.

By lunchtime the
king had had another idea.
"If the knight is too old, he can send his
son," he said.

"Does he have a son?" asked Oliver.

"Don't make things difficult!" said the king.
"If the knight and his son won't kill the dragon
. . . they can roast on my next barbecue!"

"That's not very nice," said Oliver.

The king smiled.

"My son, that is the best bit about being
king," he said. "You don't have to be nice."

2 The old knight and the new

The king's men went to see the old knight. The dragon had been that way too. The fields were black. Houses were smashed. Rivers were dry. People begged for food and water, but the king's men passed them by. They didn't want to stop. They wanted to get back to the safety of the castle.

At last they came to the old knight's house.

"You have to fight the dragon," said the king's men.

"But I'm too old," said the knight.

"Well, send your son to fight," said the men. "If not, the king will roast you on his barbecue."

"But I don't have a son," protested the old knight.

It was too late. The king's men had gone.

The old knight didn't have a son, but he did have a daughter, Harriet. Harriet was clever and brave. The old knight was very proud of her. She was angry when she heard about the king's men.

"How dare they ask you to fight the dragon!" she said. "What a coward and bully that king is." Then she smiled.
"But never mind, I've got a plan!"

Harriet went to her room. She took out her sword. It was the sword that her father had used to fight dragons when he was young.

Harriet sat down in front of her mirror. She held up her ponytail and shut her eyes. "Goodbye Harriet," she said and chopped off her hair.

She opened her eyes and smiled. "Hello, Harry!" she said. "Now for a bit of dressing-up."

3   Under attack

Back at the castle there was trouble. People
were banging at the gates.

"Let us in! The dragon's coming!" they
shouted.

The hills glowed red with fire. A cloud
of smoke hung in the sky.

The dragon was out. He was furious with
hunger and thirst. He was eating anything
that moved, and burning anything that didn't.

The king was nowhere to be seen. Oliver
was doing all the work.

"Open the gates!" ordered Oliver. "Give
the people food and water. Then get ready
to defend the castle."

Where was the king? Oliver ran all over the castle, looking for him.

He found him at his computer.

"Quick!" called Oliver. "The dragon's coming . . ."

"Sh!" said the king. "In a minute. I'm at the good bit."

Two knights were jousting on the computer screen.

"But this is real!" shouted Oliver. "We need you NOW!"

"I'm busy, can't you see?" said the king. "You deal with it." His eyes were glued to the computer screen.

Oliver was about to argue, but a *ROAR!*
boomed through the castle. The dragon
was at the castle gates!

Oliver ran to the castle walls.

"Take cover," he called to the villagers.

"Get your swords," he called to the
king's men.

He grabbed his sword and shield. There
was no time for armour.

The king's men stood there, gaping. They
weren't used to real fighting. Well, not
off-screen anyway.

"MOVE!" shouted Oliver. The king's men just stared at him.

"Look behind you!" shouted Oliver. Two giant red eyes peered over the walls. A steamy hiss made them turn.

"Aaargh!" They scrambled for their swords.

A shower of arrows hit the dragon's head, but it didn't even blink.

Its huge tongue swept along the walls like burning lava.

"Go for its eyes!" shouted Oliver. But it was too late. Two glassy eyelids slid over the dragon's eyes.

Oliver had to think, and think quickly. This dragon was strong. It was powerful. But it must have a weak spot. His mind raced back to the book of *Daring Deeds*. Then he remembered!

A dragon's heart is under its left wing.

But how could he possibly reach it?

King Max sighed. It was getting noisier and hotter.

"Why is it so hot in here?" yelled the king. "Open the window!" But nobody heard. "I have to do everything myself," said the king.

He flung open the window.

"Shut up!" he yelled. The dragon turned to look at the king. The king shouted to his men, "Kill that . . ."

The dragon breathed a huge flame. CLANG! The king's crown fell onto a pile of ash.

"Hey! Dragon!" It was Harry the knight.

Oliver looked over the walls. He blinked.
The dragon turned to see who was brave
enough and stupid enough to fight him alone.

"Stand and fight!" shouted Harry.

"*ROAR!*" The dragon was ready to smash
this knight to pieces. But the knight suddenly
thrust a sword into its tail. The tail was
pinned to the ground.

The dragon roared
with pain and anger.
    It twisted and turned but it
could not get free. It hurled fire at the
knight. It swiped with its claws. But the knight
was too quick and dodged away.

Oliver and his men cheered. But it wasn't
over yet.

"Get the dragon up to the walls again,"
shouted the knight. "Leave the rest to me!"

Oliver hesitated.

"Go on," shouted the knight. "I'll go for its heart!"

In a flash, Oliver saw the plan. He climbed onto the wall. He shouted at the dragon. He waved his sword. He threw stones. His men looked at each other. Had he gone mad?

The dragon reared up. But just as Oliver felt its burning breath, Harry plunged a sword deep into the dragon's heart.

The dragon fell. The people cheered. The knight took off her helmet and looked at Oliver. Her eyes sparkled.

"Hi! I'm Harriet," she said.

Oliver's heart missed a beat.

"I'm . . . " he began, but his words were lost as the cheering people carried them both shoulder-high round the castle walls.

That night, there was a great party at the castle. There was feasting, singing and dancing. The dragon was dead and the people had a new hero – and heroine – to celebrate.

The rest is history. Oliver and Harriet got married and became king and queen. They ruled wisely over a kingdom that was never troubled by dragons again.

In years to come, the story of Oliver and Harriet was written down. They were the last entry in the ancient book of *Daring Deeds*.